The writer has always been fascinated by language, specifically metaphors, and how they can profoundly impact the human experience and depict a single emotion in infinite streams of expression. He has been influenced by such drastically different writers—Gibran, Rumi, and Bukowski—and molding those three influences to create a unique writing style has been his ultimate goal in his literary approach.

SOMETHING LIKE POETRY

"A Story of a Damaged Writer"

Ahang Ashti A.

AUSTIN MACAULEY PUBLISHERS™

LONDON · CAMBRIDGE · NEW YORK · SHARJAH

A CIP catalogue record for this title is available from the British Library.

ISBN 9781035871933 (Paperback)
ISBN 9781035871940 (ePub e-book)

www.austinmacauley.com

First Published 2024
Austin Macauley Publishers Ltd®
1 Canada Square
Canary Wharf
London
E14 5AA

I dedicate this, full-heartedly, to the unfortunate damaged people who are still roaming this planet with their wounds and past baggage. I hope these words relate; I hope these lines give you hope, and I hope you find the closure towards an epiphany and join me in this healing journey as well. We all deserve that.

And to her.

I'd also like to show my immense appreciation to Marwa Koofe for creating all the impeccable artwork that compliments the poetry of this book and to Maha Sarchil for creating the book cover's artwork.

My acknowledgment is definitely towards heartbreak, as strange as it sounds, but it was indeed the main artery that these words flooded from.

TABLE OF CONTENTS

PREFACE

In *Something Like Poetry*, I have attempted to reflect on the journey of a damaged poet toward awakening, sentimental breakthrough, and trauma healing. It depicts a real transformation of personal experience and how I translated that process into writing.

1. I, WRITE

I guess writing had been in love with me long ago
without my notice
Like a one-sided lover who would pay a visit every
six months
But it seemed like she didn't want to leave like she
always did this time
I didn't mind
She would never hurt me; she'd accept my most
terrifying flaws
So I decided to settle with her, with Writing
We agreed on almost all the terms except for one
She would allow me to orgasm all my thoughts into
her
On the condition of never mentioning my past lovers
I agreed, knowing I would eventually cheat on her!
There was a stain of blood on the paper sheet, my
bed with her
From the papercut she stung me with earlier
It looked like a seal mark for an agreement contract
So I signed, "Him."

2. THE SOUND OF YOUR CRUMBLING

You lay there with your skin
I lay there with my fling
Your heart is elsewhere
And so are my thoughts
Two confused bodies; a rib cage that imprisons
deteriorating lungs and a dysfunctional heart
Shattered shards of glass
From a vessel that once used to carry your dreams
They cut deep with every emotional breath
Forced you to breathe numb, avoid feeling
Fingertips drew all over your face
Marks left by those who wiped your tears as they
departed
I see a pile of the wreckage of a human
But I can still visualize the statue of beauty you
used to be;
Still, among all the ashes, the tears, the damaged
parts
And the cold touch of your buried pain
After all, it was I who demolished you
And it was the sound of your crumbling that awakened
me.

3. THE GAZE OF TRAUMA

And as he gazed into her eyes
With a bitter shiver trembling through his heart
He said, "I know that I am the source of your sorrow;
I know you are the source of my joy."
How contradicting!
She looked at him with eyes that would melt rock
from the guilt it radiated in him
She said, "I am a prisoner."
She wanted to be free.
He was screaming, "I want you to fly!" but he was
grabbing her too hard
Rocking her back and forth like a lunatic while
uttering those words
She couldn't understand a word
He finally got it; his rage went still
With a breeze of reality hitting his tired face, he
said, "This is it!"
And he let go of her.

4. I AM EMPTY

I am empty
And that's not the sad part
The fact that I have to get used to it
Is the most depressing
I am sensing my human part leaking out of the
vessel body that contains it
It is suicide that you did not commit yourself
Bleed out, and I cry, trying to rehydrate my dry
heart
In vain.

5. THE BURIAL OF THE PAST

What they have taught us about the past is that
it is meant to be buried
Yet they never told us that it has to be dead first
before doing so
They never told us it would dig its way out of the
ground and haunt us for not giving it a proper
burial!

6. THROB

Throb, my exhausted heart
Keep beating as the end is about to start
Let's raise our glasses full of gods' nectar and blood
And cheer goodbye to misery and penetrating darts
We've come a long way
The battle seems to be over
For us and ego are now finally apart!

7. XANAX

So what was your cure?
"210 pills of sertraline;
A pile of Xanax;
And a pulse of hope."
What's the use of hope?
"Fuel"
What for?
"The heart."
What are you talking about?
"What runs you? Is it your ambition?"

8. PAGES

I rip pages off, one after another
Until I encounter that one page
That ripped my heart apart
And I go quiet
So does my pen
A blank moment of silence...

Paying its respect
To the birth moment of the poetry in its holder.

9. Her Thorns

I got used to her thorns penetrating my skin
Every time I try to touch her
The tolerance my body built against that pain made
me numb as fuck!
The heart still aches though
It is not made to be obedient to the mind
It will ache, ache, and ache, yet never seem to learn
It just isn't equipped with a tolerance-building
mechanism; what a sucker!
This is precisely why it loves again, a fall after
another like it is always spring ahead; what a fool!
But hey,
Never take that foolishness for granted.

10. Aching Mesmerization

There is this aching feeling that craves to touch
your soul beyond your skin
I want to hug your spirit so bad
To kiss your voice, dance with your laughter
I miss the lover you imprisoned inside your heart
That only liquor cracks its cage open
When you are no longer sober enough to guard it
It sneaks out and comes rushing toward me
This is why I am intoxicated with love the next
morning
While you wake up not remembering who you were!

11. In the Company of Other Lovers

In the company of other lovers
I was watching them with a smile
Because in my mind, in the back of my head
We were mirroring them
Shadowing every hand gesture
In every street café, I spotted one
In every minute of solitude
In every poem, I wrote
And while I was lost in those imaginations
You slapped me awake and called me a creep!
A delusional lunatic who finds refuge only in fiction
Because that is the only spot left that I can still
imagine you as a lover
It is an epiphany I'll always end my love poems with.

12. Frankenstein

As I lay the pen down, staring at your eyes, I don't know what to say to
Touching hands that made me feel I don't know who mine belong to
Listening to a soul that has nothing to say no more
Just quiet, raw, cold contentment remains from all the wreckage
That forms us, the damaged unfortunate
So we surpass all boundaries, not in regret of who we were because we didn't want to be that either
But as the last shockwave through an already dead heart
Perhaps a Frankenstein monster to arise from us
And to slowly pick up our limbs and pieces shattered between traumatizing memories
Dark corners, we visit again
Take the tour guide
Let me show you the monument of our fall
Abandoning houses we used to curse, that used to be our graveyards
That our murderers walk around, pretending what they did was love us
To walk around now with a dead body, yet a revived soul
Pick life up once again, one shard at a time
Maybe, one day, our miracle would be becoming whole again.

13. I Was a Vampire

I was a vampire
Who hadn't drunk blood in years
On the verge of dying
Underneath my mask was blue skin and purple veins
I wooed women and preyed on their flesh
I was weeping as I ripped their hearts apart
There was a soul, so dim, within the hollow blackness
of my eyes
It wept but never stopped me hunting.

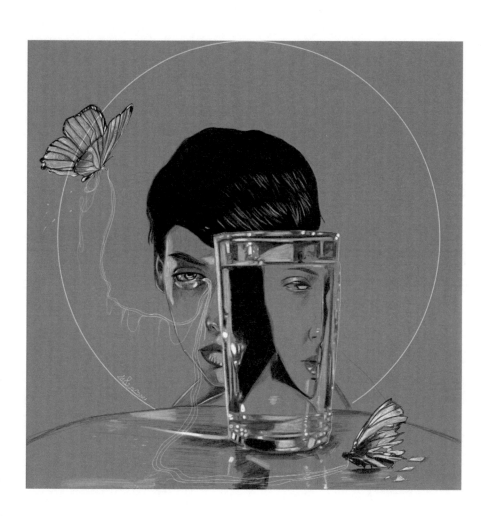

14. I Was a Werewolf

I was a werewolf who would turn into a gentleman
in daylight
And as the moon took throne on behalf of the sun
I transformed;
A vicious beast that ripped her apart at night
Yet loved her viciously, remorseful by the sun's
return.

15. I Am Human

I loved her; with my traumas, my PTSD, my insecurities,
and my troubled soul
With my ignorance and moments when I would wear
the claws of my old days again
I began to feel a heartbeat within
Each time she dropped...
I began to awake; each time she dropped...
I began to heal; each time she dropped...
A heartbeat, a body fall, a breakup.

16. I Am a Sufi

I heal to begin to see
I heal to begin to be
I heal to embrace the ego inside of me
Truth, self, and let it not anymore consume me
I realize pain is within
I realize forgiveness is for us
I realize love is within
I realize obsessions and needs are unresolved knots
that have to be untied
I is no longer an "I"; it is an "eye" that sees clashing
within means to resolve the clashes without
And from our self springs our world
How it is on the outside is how you are on the inside
To realize you have harmed none but you
By clinging to grudge
By numbing yourself with hate
Is enough to allow good to take nest in your mind,
soul, and heart
Sing as if you have just been reborn
And fly fearlessly; wings are meant to break
Yet they grow back, firmer, to maintain our flight
longer
Each time, until you have no wings left
And you can still fly; gracefully, united
Either that or you stay in the nest of victimization,
Never daring to jump off

Jump, the fall is meant to happen
We are destined to break; "till our hearts open."
So I come not because of a need for you
I come with a gift you find disbelief in now.

17. If I Were a God

And if I was a god
I wouldn't need to love you in the first place!
You would worship me unconditionally
And I wouldn't even reciprocate.
So why are you playing god with me?

18. XYZ

I am wondering why I still can't label you as an X
Maybe there isn't a specific Y
Perhaps, this isn't how this equation endZ.

19. Psychedelic – AI Poetry

I woke up at 5 AM; reached out for a bag of magic salvation
I trip to heal repeatedly, to the point that I can't remember how much skin I've shed so far
So many, so tiring to peel off of your flesh with a scraper made of your crippling PTSD
I trip to find my 'self,' and I know the consequences
That you wouldn't comprehend the idea why I carry no regrets anymore, not remorseful toward my past
Because I no longer am
I ceased to be when I decided to shed that skin threaded with regret and self-destruction
I trip to realize who I am; to find love within; to be a healthy human being; to myself before anyone else
And through that moment of inner peace, you spring out from my consciousness
Our bodies dissolving in front of each other and turning into particles of blue and white foggy energy
Twisting around each other, ascending with such graceful strength, the collision turns into a colorful masterpiece that is cosmically immortal

To leave such an anecdote of a love story that rises from the ashes of damaged people that cured their way towards love; is eternal love
I heal to love myself; I heal to love healthy; I heal to love you clearly, without insecurities, without the glitches
I am finally ready to do this healthy, but you don't have the heart for it now, not yet.

20. The Physics of Love

My physics teacher used to tell me that only opposite
magnet poles can attract each other
But I used to disagree
Probably because I hated physics
Or just my impulsive nature to go against what is
set and confirmed
So I dwelled into similar poles
And they kept pushing me distant
I pushed it a few notches further
Till my pull drive toward that person
Was stronger than the push force
But I always had to put a 150% effort to be able to
get close enough to touch that physically impossible
collision
With time, I taught myself how to maintain that
balance
Hence the balance had to be heavier from my side;
every single second of that opposing attraction,
the paradoxical pull
Yet I kept going, at times forgetting to put that
extra effort
Thinking that person would give an extra 25%, and
I could finally rest my hectic body
But my physics knowledge was obviously poor
So I was pushed miles further

Every single time I tried to rest my body a bit
Every single time I lowered my armor
So I hated my physics teacher
Not the pusher
Because it wasn't their fault
That they weren't aware of how I could even resist
that long
in the first place
So I decided to revisit my teacher years later
He asked, "Are you still going against the laws of
nature?"
And I smiled and said, "Not anymore."
His grin was of satisfaction
My smile was of a wrecked disappointment
Therefore, I decided, from that moment on, that I
would find
Love within, first
So that my heart would only attract
Frequencies of the magnetic field alike, aligned.
Then I took astronomy as a creed of love, cosmically
indulged in it
And fuck physics!
Because those who abide by its rules are the faint-
hearted, and love needs courage and bravery
To be unconditional requires stronger power than any
magnetic pole. It is divine; it cannot be engineered.

21. Dear Beloved

You don't get what it means to say you cannot and will not be a mistake, a past.

Even if we are separate.

Your almost-empty perfume bottle I must preserve from heat; so it wouldn't evaporate, as you did.

These lines don't hit home; they hit heart that the soul tortures, saying: "You never listened until it was late, for her, as her fountain of hope dried — like the perfume bottle she left on the doorstep of your torment."

So the aroma of your scent lingers in the memory cells of my brain, as well as the love garden of my soul

Roses you've planted while I was stabbing you to bleed, to water the roses; so that by the time I get to inhale their scent, the aroma of your blood had already killed you—one droplet at a time; the metaphoric rain of awakening.

Give me another perfume bottle; this time, I won't need to absorb the object that represents you; I've awakened already. Can't you see the bloodstains I left walking out of that garden next to your grave?

The red stains are fading the more I walk away from that past, where I as well hate that murderer as much as you do, perhaps a bit more than you hate him.

Hence why I panic at every single mention of something I ripped the metal plates off of, every single one hand-picked without anesthesia, where my ego was numb and my heart awake.

Give me another bottle, and I will sip it this time, piss it all over him.
Because I am burying him next to your corpse, that fucking altar of traumas, the mass murder of damaged arteries.

So leave him buried, chant your farewell prayers on your grave, and let me burn that garden down to its last seed, only allow the seldom beautiful memories to flare into smoke, cleansing themselves from damaged hearts that used to produce them. That used to take them for granted, toxically unaware.

Get out of that garden and set fire to it as I did instead of sitting in that same spot beside the limbs of your tombstone, crying, weeping, shouting, and screaming, why, WHY? And to answer why is to rip my heart off and toss it on your tomb so that you can eat it out, and that anger-filled hate of yours has finally embraced its right to revenge.

So do you want to take a deadly bite? Or do you want to heal?

Because my "why" was my father's face, and I kissed it forgivingly.
When you finally get up and leave there for your sake, you will see that I have built a statue called "The Goddess of Healing" a few miles away from where you linger, with your letters engraved... And I have left after I had bowed enough times to finally say: I have gracefully paid my debt and condolences, but most importantly, my gratefulness.

Whether you finally decide to come to this place or not, the only remaining will be the trail of my healed steps. I waited as much as my 'self' allowed me. One day, it would make sense that forgiveness is actually from within, not an approval stamp in the other person's hand!

So the only thing that remains is the engraved letters of your name, a tattoo on the skin hovering over my heart. And it no longer bothers me at all. You are valuable to me, still. Your memory can humbly occupy that space of my flesh and skin.

I can finally say that I cherish your existence even if it wasn't fused with mine.

I am sorry if I couldn't resurrect you in return, believe me, I have tried to my bones, and if I had kept trying, they would've broken one bone after another uselessly. Therefore, I wish you the bravery to face your within.

I hope you find healing within.

22. A Vulnerable Pride

Well, I've been pondering in the swamp of my alien
thoughts
I undress my body naked and expose my heart to life
without the rib cage it is meant to be protecting
I am friends with the knife tips that want to
penetrate me
I leak blood like waterfalls as a way of cleansing
my cycle of sanity
I refuse to close up
I want to stay tender like a tangerine, peel me off
with almost no effort
And if you dare to ask me why?
Well, would you rather I give you the bitterness
of my seeds
Choke you on my ego
Scratch your self-esteem with permanent marks
And juggle your insecurities like entertaining balls
for the crowd you surround yourself with?
I decide to be vulnerable on a daily basis
Each day, I sign a template vowing to stay wide open
That god updates only when he is sober
Because I've seen him on his bad days
And I decided to be the voice of righteousness on
his behalf

At the times when his glass bottom is the farthest he can see.

I wouldn't justify my filth for the mistakes of my superior

That is why, in the terms and conditions of this state of mind

The first article is 3000 lines on how nobody is responsible for your being but you

I read them, one letter at a time

This time, with an open heart and a numb ego

Because I could no longer withstand turning my ignorance into a blaming mirror

Stare at the reflection of what I've built myself with my own hands

Then blame the construction engineer

Was it god? Was it my upbringing? Was it me?

But does it even matter?

The fixing is inevitable

Then you ask, but what about people? They can be hurtful

Well, if you hurt me

I will look at you from down below

And reach out my hand with a plate on

And tell you, my friend, have the crumbs of empathy and kindness left

I am already full; you need it more than I

Because I don't see the harm as an act of strength

It is merely how much you hate yourself
That has taken a demonized character
You market around unwillingly
Until it encounters someone who wears their heart
as their vision ray
Instead of ego goggles that respond to your hatred
at the same rate of self-destruction
To comfort your dysfunctional state!
But I can no longer offer that
I don't translate your over-squeezing handshake as
the muscle strength of your self-esteem
I see empty gaps, dark holes that pull you and
scatter you around like a puppet
And I have no option but to feel empathy
Because
I was there one day, and you and I both know how
disgusting it is to dine in the same filthy place
By the same filthy cooks
And have the same filthy food
Of your goddamn creation
Every single time
So tear off that template, and start writing your
own.

23. The Corner of
Her Cheek

I seldom make wishes lately
But the only wish that permanently resides in the
back of my mind
The depth of my cortex
The corner of my heart
Is you, and it still is
Shadowing my spirit
Uttering in my subconscious
Screaming in my guts
The same epiphany over and over
I feel
A fading drum that used to synchronize with my
heartbeat
Dimming the lights she hung on my soul tree
As it felt like Christmas in my stomach when we met
You see, I only got to see butterflies around you
I had trapped some in a glass case and put them on
top of my obsessive attachment shelf
I want to break that glass, grab those butterflies,
and hand them back to you
I feel
An aching void yet a comforting home
A papercut, a matchstick burn
And even in the wish's improbability

I still visit that same temple
Where we first learned faith and love
Where every time we left the temple
We would tremble on our traumas again
Quarrel like twin siblings
Until we grew older and healthy, you just didn't wait
You left
And some wonder why I seek my other twin every single day
I'll tell you a secret
I still visit that temple at times
Alone
To be mesmerized by the scent of the memories
Still stuck on the torn curtains
Lingering in the rusty windshields
Hanging from the edge of empty vases
To see glimpses of the only missing piece
That I can invite into my living now
Healthy, glowing, and holy
To watch freckles
Forming on the skin of her hands
And on the corners of her cheeks.

24. To a Damaged Lover

I just want to ask you
How much longer are you going to keep my heart
hanging on the threads of your hate?
How many more times are you going to delegate your
ego to confront me, while I sit there waiting for
you to show up?
I want to remind you, sweet girl; you are better
than this
I've drawn the edges of your soul into a canvas
made from my past sins
And I watched it catching flames that left a trail
of a word you are not yet familiar with; forgiveness
I want to ask you
Do you also have me as the breakfast of your thoughts
every morning?
Do you also have to wear glasses to stand the
brightness of pain; is that how you also manage to
walk through your days?
I would love to know, did you also debunk the theory
that time fades love away?
Did you, by chance, figure out that avoidance is
only a sign of resistance towards something meant
to be?

And you forget that when we were born, we were barcoded with the same title
From a damaged person to another, I got to be honest; we can spend all day long counting flaws on a calculator
But the sunset of blame has to sink behind the mountain of our ignorant past
And to allow the sun to rise again from the newly healed hills
Where self assigns spring this time to rebuild what autumn just expressed and grieved on
So I excuse myself, for whom I used to be
To embody who I've been molded into in the present
Have you noticed that the only thing that survived, yet left injured in our wars, was the memories?
I turn them into fortune cards because I want to trick myself into convincing my mind that every time I draw a card,
It will be a happy nostalgic epitome
And maybe, perhaps someday, I draw one card, and you appear
Like my everyday daydreams,
Like a background music
Played by the orchestra of my life
Listen
They say silence is at times stronger than words, well...
Sigh...
Let's talk when you are ready.

25. Poetic Psychology

You see I am not a psychologist
But I understand what trauma means
What PTSD can do to a human being
I know many unfortunate people can inherit that
same trauma from those who suffered it
So for every time you called me mentally sick
Maybe you should've invested that time and effort
in building a time machine instead
Went back to the time when my father had my head
under his foot, repeatedly smashed against the floor
Maybe you could've told him
"Dear sir, Mr. Traumatized man
Can you please stop killing this young boy's spirit?
As your father did?
Can you please stop trying to pass your vengeance
on to this clueless creature?"
And then you come into my life, and I repeat the
same cycle
So inherit my pain, drown in my heritage of sorrow,
and wrap yourself with my planet of wounds
And take a walk through the graveyard of my
childhood
But you see
It was you who introduced me to an alien concept
It was your love that was bigger than my planet
called Trauma
That took over me as a universe, and I found myself
orbiting around a sun

Whose gravitational pull I knew I didn't deserve
I was ignorantly intoxicating you
And you refused to cast me away to that black hole
I came from
So what does a damaged corpse do in favor of your
divine generosity?
Takes a knife, slits its heart open
Let's dive in; let's see where the wounds lead
Let's do what my father didn't dare to do—
Face my trauma
So I picked up every single wound that deformed
my concept of love
That crippled my kindness
That made me become friends with victimization
That ripped my childhood apart
That made me hurt everyone that I ever loved because
that's how love was communicated to me
And now, I have a museum called the "Healing Spot."
I invite people, without an admission fee, without
a ticket
To come and take a tour
To see my old traumas hung on walls with flower
frames
My sad stories recited with hopeful music in the
background
And my childhood portrayed with threads made of
my veins
And as they reach the end of the aisle, there is a
statue of Gaia
A scene where she has her hand laid on my head, my
tears made of wax

And that's the epitome
That's where it hits them
We must accept what has happened
We must embrace what we have become
And we must forgive ourselves for having experienced
it
Then we move on
We heal
One part at a time
Many might wonder why I have to subject myself as
the experiment sample
Because I would've done anything to have had a
healing hand reach out to me at the time I most
needed
I would've given away 10 years of my life in exchange
So that I could love you healthy when you most
needed it
Before it was late
Before I had drained your hope
I would've done anything for that opportunity to
have come earlier
Now, I impulsively run toward people who show a
glimpse of the trauma
And I bring out my sharpener
I trim their claws, gently
And I say. "Do not hurt those you love because of
the hatred that grew within
Do not repeat my unfortunate fate."
That's why I panic at every breakup I hear of
I rush towards every vulnerable creature on my
way like a lifeguard

I risk myself to rescue others from the ignorance
I used to be consumed by, unwillingly
Because that fate is harsher than death.

26. The Confessions of a Self-Taught Healer

I want to cut to the chase
And enough of beautifying pain
I honestly would've slit my wrist long ago
If it wasn't for this blank page I take as a refuge
So I choose to pick up a tired pen rather than a sharp razor
I splatter the seeds of my agony on these pages
Hoping they resurrect on the soil of art rather than regrow on me
You see, I was born into a traumatized damaged family
So I had to carry that heritage with pride
And I looked around; my fate wasn't really different from the other kids in my neighborhood
So I grew up with a stick next to my bed instead of a teddy bear
Because I was taught that facing our fears is done through violence
And we cannot hug our insecurities away
I was taught that kindness is only shown in funerals
When we have already killed our loved ones from deprivation

And we run into the tunnel of life, seeing the light at the end
With an oblivious smile, yet unaware that we brought our monsters with us
So we feel the blessing of the light ahead
Yet unwillingly act upon the monsters we don't see
And we run into lovers that are drawn to the similar colors of the scenes of our past
Because we can now relate to the shape of our wounds and not feel lonely
Perhaps, this is why the only person we would feel that depth with
Is a person who's dived into the exact corners of hell that we have
And instead of seeking inner redemption
We seek salvation in one another
Self-love is an alien term at the time
Then we eat each other out
Since our monsters found a host who is familiar with the shape of our claws
And is willing to embrace us, and our demons clash, because demons don't play monopoly, they play destruction
In that equation, there are always two roles; the victim and the oppressor
We are left with glimpses of the light and mountains of damaged arteries

One day, I woke up from the sedation of my ego, where
My DNA told my ego, "It is enough. Your defense
mechanism is preventing scenarios of your childhood
from reoccurring.
But hurting your present far more."
When I woke up, I was just three steps away from
the end of the tunnel
And for the first time, I looked, with my heart
awake and my ego numb
To see a lover I never had met before in my true
form
But they had spent years trying to run away from me
I realized I had my grip and claws penetrating her
since my ego had her hostage
It was the fear of facing my childhood's death that
I never dared to attend the funeral of
It had immortalized me by numbing my heart, blinding
my sight, and forming me into something I am not
None of us are
And I weep, waterfalls, all of a sudden
Looking at my lover's wounds, knowing my hands
have committed these acts
Looking at myself, grieving my trauma
Looking at my watch, I see so much time has passed
in this comma
Looking at her...speechless and paralyzed
So I die, again, as an adult

But this time, I attend my own funeral, and I grieve
for months
I wake up from that shock
Through a borrowed pulse that can beat with whatever
shattered pieces left as a heart
Through a friend's glimpse of empathy
Through a voice I hear for the first time now clearly
What used to be whispers that were volumed down
by my ego
This time, my self was the speaker
It was its first time conversing with me
And it said something strange: "I was waiting for
you, and while you were distracted, I was lecturing
your heart."
It seems like our hearts and souls carry walkie-
talkies and have late-night conversations
And our egos, out of jealousy, befriend us instead
So I crawl toward the end of the tunnel
Only to realize how far I've crossed is actually a
shorter distance compared to the distance left
The tunnel light was only to show that we had a
light in us all along
It was the journey, hinting where you could land
There is a dilemma even in healing
You see, I can finally get on my feet again now,
with grace
I can walk those few remaining steps and exit the
tunnel

But I look back and see my lover still bleeding on the dark corners of that altar of trauma
I weep; I scream with all my lungs' capacity
"Come here, come!"
But their ego is still present, and I remember my friend's advice, saying, "You can't possibly speak butterfly language to caterpillar people."
But he forgot that a butterfly's heart has more empathy than it can actually withhold
That's why butterfly wings are fragile, vulnerable, and soft
Yet is never scared to land on flowers and expose itself to risk
You see, a friend told me, "Move on, save yourself!"
But they don't understand that she and I are named the same, so I am literally saving myself by saving her
You see, a friend told me, "You can't blame yourself for the deeds you committed blind."
But they don't understand that when we finally see, we take responsibility for our mistakes rather than carry the blame
You see, a friend told me, "She sees you as a walking bag of traumas!"
And I smile because I don't expect anything less from someone I crushed so many times
So I run back into the tunnel, despite the irrational sense of that action

I run towards my past; I go past my graveyards and revisit my old self, a cold corpse lying there
I am horrified by the scenes
But the light in me won't fade
And as I arrive close, I see her drawing her claws, ready to rip me to pieces
Can you blame her?
She sees me as the same old monster; because I am meeting her in the same spots those crimes were committed
Do you see the dilemma?
So I stop attempting to fight the wolverine at night time and wait for the daylight to arrive
And I turn around and see so many zombified hearts
Walking around
And I run toward them
I hug their spirits
And I slit my skin and feed them some blood
Enough to wake them back to life
Enough not to drain me out of it
And I try to revive them one after another
As if, subconsciously, each one I help heal
I feel like I have healed a fragment of her as well
Perhaps, I do this unconditionally
Perhaps, it is the duty of those who found their way
To pass on the map toward their true self to others
The only difference is, I had to create my map from pieces of my own skin

The only difference is, I was self-made
The only difference is, I was given the role of the savior hero
Because there was no one else in my neighborhood
To bother enough taking that role, none of them survived
But who saves the hero at the end of the day?
When they retire back to their nest, taking back straws of other people's pain and build up the nest higher
Was I cursed by this blessing?
Am I paying my karma in this form?
Until when?
I am honestly fucking tired!
I am honestly so sick of the word trauma that I feel like I want to puke my soul out of this body when I hear it
Wouldn't you be, if you were born into trauma, grew up acting on it ignorantly unaware, and still, to this day suffer from its consequences even after conquering most of it
A friend once told me, "It is because we were so damaged that we got addicted to fixing."
And I thought about it
It is actually true; some traumas will never leave
There are some tumors that turnout benign
And shape us into our finale
This is why when my body started mending its wounds, and when it got to the point of mending the wound of your departure

I would deliberately peel off the layer on that skin again
Because I rather live with the burning pain of your memory eternally
Than let it heal and erase you from the last bits of me
Do you know how crazy it is
To love someone to the point that even when their heart reconstructs its pieces together
There is that thin slit in the middle left hollow
Like I am waiting for you to insert a coin in
So that I can finally say, "Holy shit, I am whole again!"
Some wounds are meant to stay the same as the way we carry their scars mandatorily
Otherwise, if I let that mend too, I won't reach out to anyone anymore
I won't write this way anymore; I won't have meaning anymore
And I will have only the sharp razor left as an option.

27. Poet Goggles

You said
"I'll never date a poet again; they say things they
don't mean and exaggerate how they feel"
But we both saw how your eyes glittered, hearing
words your ears are virgin to
Discovering beautiful land stones on your body
that you've never set sight on
And being loved in corners of you that you didn't
know possible to be seen by another
Let's be honest; you rarely won't fall for a mind
that asks you, "What's your aura's color?"
That stares at your shoulder blades like they are
paintings
Sightsees through the very same physical scars
that you labeled as imperfections
Has a mindful conversation with your insecurities,
as if they are children of his own
Wants to glue every bit of you together
So you won't fall apart
You won't be heartbroken
You won't, in the same way, become a poet
So it is not the poet you fell in love with in this
human
It is not the words
It is because of the way he decides to picture you
Is the same way you want to be.

28. The Wink

I remember precisely when her fingertips started
growing cold on my skin
When her lips tasted numb
When her words started speaking with an empty tone.
Perhaps, when she was saying, "All things are
temporary."
I had hoped she'd understand me when I replied,
"Yes, but love needs consistency."
So she drew me as a painting with a fade-able paint
And I carved her on my heart, with permanent scars
So we confused each other because one has learned
to love to the extent
That when the heart is about to nest the other
They fly away
And the other had a settled heart and saw forever
in her eyes;
Now I understand what the wink meant.

29. The Blacksmith

And today, I wanted to decide to say I've had enough
Because Guilt put his hat on and departed
And Karma checked off the last item of its to-suffer
list, looked at me, and said goodbye
And Trauma was a toxic close friend I had to cut
ties with
I want to invite my heart out to dinner
And have the closure talk with instead
The conversations I had wanted to share this time
weren't long or demanding
I would say I am starting to love myself now
You actually achieved something that other women
rarely can
Which is to fix a man;
A damaged one."
So your mind fell out of love with me, not just
because of the traumatized deeds
But because you are not drawn to someone who no
longer needs repairing with your "toolbox love"
I know that your life has turned you into a blacksmith
And you needed someone with untightened screws,
their metal spikes sharp
So you can tighten my screws with your need's spinner
Hit my iron edges until they are turned to something
that doesn't cause permanent cuts
But you forget that when you brought me to your
workshop

I was secretly adding my touches to my sculpture
heart when you retired to bed tired
I would cry with empathy knowing how tired you
get every day; the fact that I knew
You are bandaging your hands as you go to your
room
This is why you would pass out on your bed
Not hearing the pounding sound of my own work at
nights
And I molded myself into something different
And I was brave enough to weld those screws
And turn them into something acceptable, so that
when you came back
The next morning
You were surprised that you didn't feel bumps as
you glid your hands on my outer shell
It was just suddenly a smooth touch
And you would suddenly stop...
I guess you never even imagined the work you were
doing had an ending
You just didn't know what to do
So my question is, can you please explain
Why do you hate this sculpture that you helped
build?
This poem will be long again, so simply;
Thank you, and I love you through soul; I would be
grateful to have your friendship
Because, if you could, that means you indeed overcame

the impact I left
When you had taken the contractor role of rebuilding a mess
You should've known; putting your hands into a mess, will get you messy as well
And when you put on your uniform, you expect it to get stained
But I know you can't because you aren't over me
And you are trying to keep your head above the water as much as possible
Swim as hard as you can
Drink it away
Avoid looking me in the face
Block me everywhere
Delude yourself into thinking I don't exist
And post hundreds of threads and show people that hate and unforgiveness are powerful tools to overcome this
But it doesn't work like this, child
Don't misinform them about how to let go, don't turn them harsh
You will get tired of swimming, not very soon
But not very late either; the dive is going to happen
This isn't about what happened
Nor my awakening
It is about you
Your soul speaks to me; this is when your ego is numb
When you are in that cabin, alone

When your phone is not distracting you
Your overwhelming work isn't keeping you busy
No longer drawn to boys that need fixing
You are terrified by that moment of silence
Because you know if, for one minute, you quiet your
mind with its traumas
Your soul will speak angrily
Of what you are causing it
This isn't about me; it is your only life
You are ending, and now because I love, I feel, I
see, healthy
I come to you to save you from the same mistakes
that used to consume my self's entity
Heal your heart, for you, but kindly
Hate can never do that
Only love can.

30. Dear Confused Girl

A mature man seeks an evolved woman that embraces
her human part before her gender
He observes your energy
How you vibe with the universe
And what frequency you emit
Because your estrogen and pheromones are not the
pulling poles of his attraction
And testosterone is not his driving force toward you
So dear confused girl, kindly evolve first, love
your self,
Then find a mature, evolved man
Because only then would you seek love, not from a
need of lacking it yourself
But because you want to share it with someone who
has built it in themselves as well
You will finally stop falling for boys that flirt
with only your physical features
You no longer will say: all men are trash
Because you will finally realize that, at that time,
you just kept picking those who couldn't see beyond
your skin!

31. To My Daughter-to-Be

Dear child,
I want you to listen to your father
When you one day read this poem
You'll understand why I raised you so
I am sorry, but I won't get you pink and purple
Barbies to play with
I'll get you children books; I'll get you learning
games
I won't let you get brainwashed into adopting a
social norm definition of what a female should be
But I'll make sure you grow to see the difference
between cloning what they define
And finding your own definition
Of what you want to be
I will give you love; healthy, free, unbound
Unconditionally
So you won't seek in men what your father lacked
I recognize my image's impact on you since birth
So I will show you floods of emotions
I won't be the dad that sees your tears but cannot
approach because I am supposed to be tough
I won't allow you to sign a contract that you are
my honor's holder, I won't ask you to take careful
steps
Because I know suppression and tyranny we rebel
against
You will float free, only love to be given to you
as my desired duty

I will teach you what humans are
How they behave, and why
But most importantly, how their damaged parts move
them in such distorted dance
I will dance with you as you grow, yes, you will glow
And you shall shine on all dance floors
Because you are natural, you radiate with an
un-fabricated heart
With a vulnerable beauty and the lighthouse of love
So they will gather around you
Like how night insects gather around the light
And I'll teach you how to reach out to them
And you will teach me how you healed them
Because your father mended his broken heart
While you can act on an undamaged one
I would love to see the goddess you would become
And tell them, show them, teach them
That a female is human first
That gender is a secondary identity
To who you are
Prove to them that you can be original
You can be your true self, without what they copy
Yet still, attract eyes that crave the bravery to
drop their masks too
Because those who don't fit in, stand out the most
Yet you stand out tall, you stand out firm
And they will get frustrated trying to shape you
Into what they are comfortable with
And you will gently push them away with your touch
And they will never be the same again
Your mother, I don't know who she is yet

But I vow to you she will be someone you look up to
And her most valuable advice will be
Make sure you put makeup on for your soul too
Beyond skin
She will tell you to put mascara on your third eye
Before you are even concerned with your lashes.

32. The Angry Poem

I don't know what the fuck I was thinking
Waiting for your validation of my healing
As if your image of me mattered more than what I
accomplished
While angels were dancing in my cleansing ceremony
I was gazing upon you from far, ignoring them
I don't know who the fuck do you think you are
But this is my angry poem
And I want to express anger as it comes
Let my healing be messy
Let it roar if it needs to
There is not a single fucking thing you can do to
change this, with your entire ego's might
I will crush it under my kindness
And brush it off with my loving self
And with all your burning desire wanting me to
prove you right
To prove to you that I am that same piece of shit
You went for in the past
So that your subconscious gets to witness that old
me it fell for
I will not give it to you
I swear to you on the sincerest corners of my soul
I will not give in to you
Even if I hold the cards in my hands
I will not change back to whom I hated
Even if I could get you back that way

I vow to you on my existence; you will cry your
heart out
If not soon, if not ever, your angels will, on your
behalf
And you will know that the phenomenon of facing
your inner self
Is done by a few men scattered on this earth
I happen to be one, you ignorant asshole
My value to myself is millions of star years ahead
of what you set for me
It is not my fault you are trapped by your ego
When I come forward to you without mine
It is not my fault you decide to remain in the dark
It is not my fault you are not brave enough to face
yourself
It is not my fault I healed beyond guilt
That I forgave myself
And honestly, fuck you if you ever degrade my
change
Even if you don't believe in it
Even if they can't convince you of it
Even if you live off not accepting it
Even if it feeds the fireplace of the hate corner
you created
Thinking that only hatred can generate heat for
your dead heart
And you wonder why you are this way, every day

staring at a mirror to observe something you are not
Fucking give in to love already; what the fuck are you waiting for?
Love yourself, for fuck's sake!
All right, go ahead, try it out, and see those who struggle to conquer themselves
And give it some time
And watch the ugly demons resurrect again
Because all they need is soil to grow back on
All it needs is the comfort stage to show up
Watch them
Fucking their way out of it
Drinking their way through it
Wave their penises around
Pierce their vaginas
Running away from aloneness
Build fake alpha-male statues on the walls of their insecurities
You forget that those are the same supposedly strong men that come to me for salvation
Because they know, whether they admit it or not, I have learned how to fuck my own ego
Which is, technically, the woman of their dreams to sleep with
Instead of being strap-on fucked by her every day
You will know, by heart and mind
That I was the bravest man you've ever known

I was braver than my father and yours and any man
you will run into
As long as you refuse to dive into yourself
As long as you brand victimization as a Louis Vuitton
purse, you carry with you every day
As long as your makeup layers get thicker
To avoid showing the expressions of how your soul
really feels
Trapped
You will realize that what you witnessed in me in
those 2500 days
Was a miracle seldom takes place in a damaged human
That you were a part of shaping a masterpiece from
broken glass
No edges that cut anymore
But piss me away; pretend you never felt for me
Yet the audience is sometimes aware of the outcomes
more than the writers
So perhaps it is true, to stop running after you to
save you
And go back to myself
Until that day comes when the table flips
I will have already flipped you off.
Don't be fooled
I am still full of testosterone
To the point that it leaks out of me
That's why my pen writes this "ballsy"

And I am so "tough"
That I face my pain
Rather than run away from
Like a "pussy"
And as my anger fades
I honestly wish you well, still
I pray that you find yourself
I wish you bravery
Because hate is fear
And I am now fearless
And it is cute to be vulnerable
As a human being.

33. Ink Bottle

They say poetry is a well-experienced woman
You have to be very good with your pen to make
her climax
At 3 AMs, she takes a bath in my ink bottle
She offers herself to me
Invites me in
And as she spreads her sheets open
I am aroused by inspiration
And the lovemaking begins
And I write...

34. My Heart's Kingdom

I have come in peace with your love that has taken
a permanent residency in my heart's kingdom
Because I've learned to expand my kingdom, not
through conquering other hearts
But my own
So you can have that piece of land named after you
Your army can guard it for as many years as it
makes you feel fearfully safe
I have abandoned my army; I have removed all fences
and walls
And there is nothing that runs through me but a
stream of consciousness
I find myself playing a game of auditions
Where I sit with different women, mostly in coffee
shops, not whorehouses
And I subconsciously interview them to answer three
critical questions;
Have you learned how to love yourself?
Have you awakened your consciousness?
And have you surpassed your gender conditioning?

Then the reality check kicks in
Telling me, "You seek traits that didn't exist in her
The same reasons that led to that departure."
So maybe I am terrified to repeat that cycle
So those conditions narrow the candidates' number
down by far
And they expand my search diameter by thousands
of miles
So I study their horoscopes
I analyze their personalities and behaviors
And I can almost predict every course of the
conversation
Only to realize how heavy the impact of your
departure was
That I treat these women like test subjects
And I have visions of you, sitting on the table
behind that woman I am facing
Looking at me and smirking, whispering, "She, won't,
replace, me!"
And I know that fact...
Because I measure them through you
I look for your eye pupils within theirs
I seek a scent similar to yours
I even tell them my favorite perfume on women;
because they were all the ones I befriended on
your neck

I even look for a crooked eye, slightly smaller than the other,
I look for a scar behind the eye because I know seeing that will be a sign
Because, with all honesty, I see you divine, and I can do nothing to convince my mind otherwise
With all my intelligence, my awareness, my conscious mind, and my awakening
Perhaps, those are the same reasons I define you as such in the first place!
Oh, they are fascinated by the product I am now
They love what I am formed into
They adore this sculpture
And as I explain my story, I can see frustration appearing in their facial expressions
Until they snap and yell
Just fucking let go of her, I am here offering myself to you
Why won't you move on?
The answer is simple;
It was her who helped shape this
This, that others crave so bad
And what keeps me waiting
Is that, perhaps, sometimes
An art creator will one day go through the archive of their masterpieces

And admire that piece as much as the audience does
So I somehow, someway, still belong to you
And always will
Yet recognizing my separate entity
Eventually, I gave in. I have to be fair
Often, men don't cheat because a relationship entitles
them not to
But this is why so many fail because their hearts
aren't true
So I refuse to involve someone else
Invite them into my heart's kingdom
When I still seek you in them
But I'll always get close enough
I'll always run by those edges
Because I am forever a writer.

35. Paddle

At times, this goes a few lines beyond poetry
And the writer finds a break
Throughout all the paddling he does
Because you know, poetry
Is like attaching an old water pump to your heart
You gotta paddle for all those sensations
To gush out
And you keep paddling
Until you dry out of feelings
And there is a breakpoint
There is a climax in the storyline
It is a moment
Empty
Peace, a puff of serenity with a sprinkle of tranquility
Then the downfall
And rolling downwards
You must hit rock bottom
All over, a few times a year
Because we need material to write about
Therefore, I am my own emotions' stuntman
We embrace how life feels; entirely, for those who
just do the acting part.

36. Silhouettes

She said, "Write a poem about me."
And I can't find the words to describe a shadow
A silhouette of vails and curtains
Covering the masterpiece behind them
I see through them, but don't intend to stop passing
through
I am not looking for a heart stop in the station of
their emotions
But I get the confusion I stir
In your heart's jar
I know the right recipes, I add them, precisely
Yet
They are not for you
They are not mine either
You can see it on my face
You can read it in my teeth
And you can sense it in my absence
In my limited touch
In my conservative approach to feelings
Yet so capable of feeling
I am sorry to confuse you
Because I am as well

37. A Turn On

When I am asked by a woman what turns me on
I say
Your lipstick marks on a coffee mug after a beautiful
conversation
Your eyes not looking away from mine when I compliment
you; acknowledging that you deserve it
When I show glimpses of the space of my feelings,
and you immediately show interest in astronomy
When you recognize the complexity of my structure,
yet you want to grab every brick of me
The whole ones, the cracked ones, and even the broken
When you are drawn to the vibration of the energy
I emit, my human self
Rather than squeeze me into a package labeled as
an attractive alpha male
Because only then, I also will be drawn to you
Knowing you have a soul residing next to your
estrogen
That is what turns me on
That you can see what I am, what I am made of, the
whole ingredients, and love every bit of it, as I
love yours.

38. The Glowing Sign

I stare at this glowing sign you gave me years ago
that says "Follow your heart"
Back then, I didn't even know anatomy
You see, you somehow, someway, knew what I am, and
what I lacked even before I ever got to know myself
And I know now that there are soulmates that enter
our rooms, splatter everything around, what is
already messy
And they find a glowing coin we had lost in that
pile of our childhood incidents long ago
So you hand me this sign, hoping I do; follow my
heart
It took me time, lover
It took me time...
As mine was in pieces
I have no fucking clue
How you survived so angelic
Through your incidents early in your life
But realize, some of us take more time
Some of us have been beaten out of hope to our bones
Some of us turn harsher than expected
I just don't get it, lover, now that I do follow my
heart to the core
Now that I am all heart
Now that I meditate on this sign you gave me every
morning
Now that I have hung the sign on my chest cage, on
the rib next to my heart

On the rib, they say you were made of
That I turned it to every background picture
On every device I have
Not only the one I hold in my hand
But the one I hold in my chest cavity too
Why do you stay away?
Why aren't you here?
Why was this lesson to be learned late?
Why isn't this a reality we live and build?
I did learn faith, but I don't want to leave the temple
It is the only spot on earth, I feel
I've ever felt
This is why I can write how it is now, at this exact moment
As my eyes want to drip on this phone
Because it wants nothing but to be sincere
It rips me to pieces to see you in the dark now
It is heart-shattering that we have exchanged roles
You were me when I was dead
I am you when you were trying to revive me back from my traumas
Would I ever be able to perform that same miracle on you?
I wonder every day
I now know how you felt, not just felt
How feeling this feeling felt in its precise detail
I now know what you meant by dying every day
I know, not just know
I am aware that this is like an everyday reminder
Like an alarm clock of pain and agony

Going off in the back of my fucking head, set for each hour of the day
And at times, when I feel weaker than usual
It somehow sets itself to ring every minute
To remind me, to fuck me up
To straighten me up
To force me to be human
To slap me back to my true self
To bully my ego
To keep me tender
To iron out my behaviors
To preach to me self-control
To revive your departure
To reopen the wounds
Just in case I happened to enjoy the blessing of forgetfulness for 59 minutes
Don't ever dare to tell me I don't know how I made you feel in my past form
Don't ever dare to even think of such a thing
Because my words, my poetry, it is not just about you
It is made of you, it is made for you, it is meant for you
It is all you
And those words are not expressed
These words are ripped out of my heart, typed by my fingers
While I watch this process happen
I just shed some tears
To stir this paste
And shape it into something
That when other lovers read

They should think twice, thrice, millions of times
Before hurting someone they love
Even if it is because of their traumas
Even if they are ignorant
Even if they don't know
Even if there are 900 excuses to justify it
My poems made sure they covered all those reasons
and why not to commit them
And a few more...
Just to make sure, I save them
Because I couldn't save you
I couldn't save us.

39. Poetry and Stitches

Healing occurs within us
Poetry is a form of therapy
It is a soothing liquid you apply to your wounds
But the stitches are our job to sew
One by one
Keep applying a drop of poetry
On every stitch you are about to make
Perhaps, this is why some of us need an ocean of
writing
Till we finally get there.

40. Cutscenes

I know this scene will occur before it even has
I will be sitting with another stunt double of yours
On a rooftop
At a sunset
Dusk takes over
In mere seconds
Because the only memories I have
Are an old VCR player
That set your memories on repeat
Even with my eyes shut, I can still hear them
The volume down button is stuck
Why won't you get out of my cortex?
Let this woman that wants to battle for your throne
At least have a chance
But they draw their white flags
From the first glance
Why do you have to leave your signature on every
moment I purchase?
This beautiful creature, right in front of me
Your ghost tapping on my shoulder, standing right
behind me
I want to escape you so fucking bad
That I long gave up the idea of emptying my mind
of you
So I march towards scenes
Making remakes of our original love cutscenes
They just don't match up

They just revive an already felt feeling
They just scratch the surface of a screen
An old goddamn record play
Rust and dry clay
They are semi-real
They are just distracting me
From something
I already know
Too well, so well
That it somehow granted me the ability
To create my own life scenes
Trying to replicate
An old VCR tape
That doesn't fit in today's reality
The sun dims down
The scene goes black
The girl still wants the poet
But the poet wants you
And the scene repeats, again
Another character, another "action!"
Except for the poetry, it never stays the same
Because one day, I will write
Without using you as my ink; as always
Therefore, kindly release my pen.

41. Ink Dots

I honestly realized
That I am in love with poetry
Far more than I am with you
Because in every line
Within every ink dot
Your true features start appearing
The ones that made you a lover
But in real life, you are just a bad print
Of my own words.

42. Vagina Trophy

I was taught by traumatized men
That all boys when they become men must build a
shelf
Where we can lay the vagina trophies on top of
Every time we penetrate one
This is why we hated women
That had self-worth more than a trophy.

They taught us to take the profession of a male
whore
Voluntary
Perhaps we need to finally know
That a profound lesson a woman can teach
Is how to preserve our bodies
And only allow a selected few to enter our temples
We, men, had abandoned our religion
From the moment we started getting a boner
I was taught by a woman who knew the value of
everything
Everything I had, was cloned concepts
Deflecting from the shadows of men
That never knew the taste of love
Who had been brought up in the same neighborhood
where hatred resided in

And were taught by abuse-methodology-using teachers
Whip-using parents
And a flood of traumatized kids
Defense mechanism-ing with bullying
To subconsciously let out their pain
Holy fuck! That is a town I don't recommend visiting
So my house was right on that street corner St. PTSD
You see, some of us escape
That neighborhood
This is why you have to be patient
With a caterpillar
You need to wait out the poison
To empty his veins
Because that leap of faith
Is a declaration of death
For him
In the neighborhood we lived
Traumas gang up in territories
They make turfs in every damaged area of you
And when you want to escape
They have threatened you with death
Take a moment, realize, that if you found a man who
wanted to escape
Because of you
You were more precious than his own life to him
Save those men
Don't let them die in vain.

43. Poetic Masturbation

I want to masturbate to the shape of your flaws
Make out with your scars
Flirt with your wounds
Until they shy away and enclose
Before you uncover your skin
Let me see what you hide in your mind's box
Introduce me to your insecurities
Tell me their names one by one
And tell them, this is him,
He is here to have a talk with you
But I am not doing your own work
I am just going to teach you how the conversation
takes place
You will take notes
But don't fall—in love
I know it will be hard
Though even if you did, I would still leave
Yet you will still learn this time
Because I won't leave scars
Only lessons.

44. The Pilgrim

There is a healing spot I've built
That shelters healing refugees
I met when I was a pilgrim
And they wondered on so many occasions
Why I circle around you
Like the Blackstone of my faith
Yet I was the only one
Who worshipped you that way.

I guess you were the compass of my conscience
That gravitated my purpose
To un-ravish myself
From what wrecked me
To the point, I could wreck you
But enough tragic talks
Because I wanted you to know
That it doesn't sting anymore
Looking at your picture
It just saddens me a little
Knowing I had to unlove you
By force
Since I was overtaken by the idea
You would seek refuge in that shelter, as well
Where I can save you, ironically, from what I thought
was my wrongdoing
But if I speak you from my soul
I no longer shiver with guilt

For what my awareness level was at
In those times
I do know, that you were broken, from when I met you
And I do know, my broken parts
Knew exactly how to revive yours
And we clashed; we both fought our damaged parts
In each other
I would carry a flag of an oppressor
You would carry the flag of the oppressed
Nevertheless, we both had our armies of
Traumas that rebelled against our souls
Rather negotiate peace within
And heal
If this makes no sense to you now
It eventually will when a ray of light
Seeps into one of the cracks of your damaged heart
When you begin to heal
I'd like you to know
That in those last months you were there
You saw my first glimpses of healing
And even though I had my flares every now and then
They were acting up
Because they were performing their last acts
I'd like you to realize that I know you noticed the
change I was going through

And it is OK that you were scared, I was too
Before I change my oppressor-so-familiar tone
I'd like you to know
That those months after we departed
I was quiet for long, longer than any other 50
million times we had departed before
It made you wonder, and gave me time to continue
the healing
And when I started showing up again
I didn't want you
You were much behind, in rebuilding your heart
While I thought you had done the same
But I came back to see you
Training the same army of your traumas
Even more intensely now
And I heard you telling them, "Repeat after me
Hatred keeps you alive
Forgiveness is for the weak."
And as I tried to step in
To reach you with my new light
Trying to seep into one of your heart's cracks
Your army held me back
I cannot fight you as I used to
Don't you understand, I have abandoned my army
I am not here for war

I am not here to win against you
I just wanted to save you
From yourself
And you thought you still need to save yourself
From me
The irony is a folk song
In the background of our love story.

45. Fingerprints

After you
I meet women
I brush my thumb's skin against theirs
Hoping our fingerprints match
But are there ever matching ones?
And how come did it feel so with you?
Perhaps it was all just an illusion
Because we damaged ones
Tend to hallucinate
Sometimes for years
So I take a pause
And I realize
You never had a fingerprint
You were always anonymous
Because only you and I
Understand why.

46. A Sincere Apology

I am sorry
I know I have hurt you badly,
Even if it is past
I get to apologize now because
My fucking god, how could I?
It is horrible to reimagine
What I used to do
On so many occasions
Towards you
You were trapped
Yet
You took years of agony
For love
It is a religion you taught
I was a rebellious student
It is strange how life works
Now
I do preach the same principle
You practiced
On a lost soul
Till your own downfall
Rose them.
It really is painful to absorb this
Listen, I am sorry

I don't have any excuse
I am not saying
That was easy
It was fucking torture!

I swear just putting myself in your place in those times
Now with this empathy
I feel my heart getting stung with sharp-edged pain
I have nothing but respect for you
You have truly changed me, from the inside
You helped me
And you sacrificed your own goddamn self
Throughout the process
And I
With all sincerity
With all gratitude
Have built a permanent monument for you
Right in the center of my fucking heart
And I will spend the rest of my life
Guarding it
You deserve it
I am sorry
There are millions of trapped words
I want to tell you
There are exactly 357 heart wounds
Some still open

Some turned to scars
My trauma bullets had fired
Listen, I am not crazy!
I put a lot of work in myself, like crazy work
This is why I have learned to let go
Much lighter, much longer
Without running after you with claws
That want to nest in flesh
Those demons I tamed
You said if you truly loved me
You would let me be, for as long as I need
And I am
Leaving the only remark of love
You had visualized on that statement
Come back, when you're ready
I feel like I am, I feel like I am almost there.

47. Poor Men

Our mothers always used to say:
Why did you break that girl's heart?
As if we men are job titled as heartbreakers from birth
As if we don't have one ourselves
And when a man dares to come forward and say, What about my heart?
He is de-masculinized for mentioning a taboo
Emotions, feelings, vulnerability
These are traits that have been twisted to demean our value
I was taught by a father
That anger is the only instrument we are allowed to play our emotions on
And if anyone were out of tune, he would be called unmanly
You see, we often are sentenced to death by birth
And then we are asked why we live so carelessly
Why do we live as dead bodies?
Because it was my birthright to be responsible
For every broken heart I encounter
Rather than nourishing mine,
Noticing that it has the same function
Besides pumping blood

So we push a wagon loaded with shattered hearts
From a self-destructive town to another
Making our way through the capitals of heartbreaks
Heavier, at each stop
So who heals a broken man?
A broken woman.

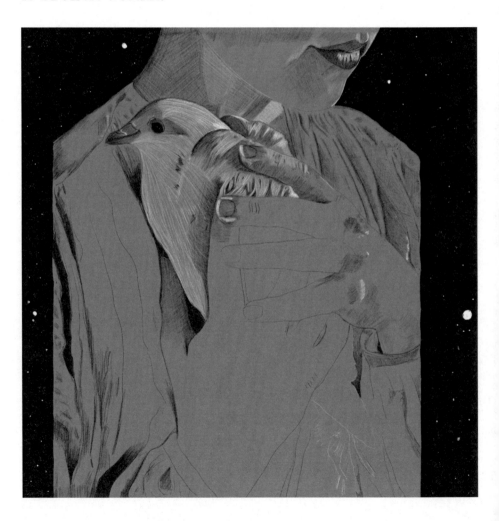

48. The Three Dots

There are three birthmarks
Sitting next to each other, aligned so well
I like how you are here not to save me
But to cherish how I stood on my feet again
Scarred yet determined
Damaged yet so well-constructed
Irresistible, you claim me to be
While I have two contradicting thoughts
Springing from hearing your claim
A reaffirming smile that shows up first
To acknowledge your compliment
Before the confused sense that I am not used to
hearing this
Because my last love career reference
Wasn't really good
Yet you choose my application
Out of many
Who applied for your healthy heart
I understand the strings of the cosmic
Which is why I had to run into three dots of a sign
To recognize the universe's heritage
To me

As it ascends you down to earth
Like I was waiting for a heavenly drop
To equip me with some unconditional touch
I was tired, you know
All these years
Begging for someone
To just understand
That I was ill
I was gasping for air
I needed an AED charge
Way before the CPR they never gave me
I've found out that there are many phases in healing
The first is when you realize
You are damaged
Some can never convince their ego to see it
The second is the tear of grief
You acknowledge that your cosmic stars
Had an unfortunate relationship with your luck
The third is to pick yourself up again
Who else, on your behalf, would do it?
And the fourth is not to allow your anger and hate
Consume it
The fifth is to stitch yourself back together
Threading threads into your skin through pitch
blackness

Which might cause new scars to close the old ones.
But this time not permanent
Then you allow yourself to heal
Finally
And from there on, you keep adding a stitch
At a time
Yet the healing story of a damaged person is ever-going
It is always lacking
A cracked vessel mended together with glue
Leaving trails of scars
Glorifying monuments
Recognized milestones
In every curve, in every angle
You stare at
The masterpieces
We become
Which is why
Our kind
Always finish their stories
With three dots...

49. Bed Sheets

When you and I finally take refuge in bed
God takes a pause from all the chaos in the world
And just watches us melt into each other, again
Because we are those few
That reminds him how
Humans are still capable
Of creating magic
From the simple fusion of compatible skins
This is why our bed sheets are made from angels'
feathers
And our mattress is a canvas of art
That our body movements paint on
And our pillow is where we keep all our promises
In that wonderland
So we stopped asking ourselves
Why hours turn to seconds
Why it gets better every single time
And we just embraced the gift we've been given
I love you the most in bed
And not for just the above reason
But because you are the most vulnerable there
And you give me beautiful promises
That I know you won't fulfill
The moment you step out of that temple

The moment that ritual stops
I love you more in bed, as a location
Not an act
Because you build that home with me
On the springs of the mattress
And even though they wiggle in instability
All the ingredients are there
Stirred and mixed
Whenever we decide to go for another spin
But, will you ever dare to love me when we step out
of that bed?

50. Narnia Kingdom

She said, my friend, when will this stop
When will I stop giving away one-way tickets
Destination—My heart
With big discounts
To people who still cheap out of buying it
I compensate so much
That the flesh melts on bones
Drips all over those victims
And just builds a thicker crust
On top of their senseless skins
Because, I am aware, I comfort them
To the point that taking me for granted
Was a contract I signed on their behalf
Don't try to blame me, my friend
I have washed away my shame
Pride is a pair of sandals
I wear it when I take my daily walks
In my modesty beach
So don't you dare to point your finger
At your own reflection
Even though your heart is a little thicker
I see it is made from the same ingredients as mine
Isn't it funny we run into similar characters
It is the same game, we are the hero

And we must save, must give
Nobody gives a shit how the hero feels
That is how they are built
That is their curse
And each time we are given another medal of heartbreak
The purple hearts hung on our suits
For all the inner wars we fought
For all the battles we won
And as we retire to start healing ourselves
Another damaged person
Is thrown at our house porch
And our conscience is not designed
To not answer the door
Dear stranger, step inside
But this time, I am not expecting you to stay
Yet that doesn't prevent the heart from getting
attached
I won't strip love out of its autonomy
Let it do what it is made for
This is why I am human
This is why you need me
And this is why I need to save you
Because as self-sacrificing as it sounds
You will come to my grave
And say your prayers
A grateful heart
Always out-wins the ego, eventually

Save your tears, I was there begging you
Your tears on my grave tombstone
Mean shit now
My heart was in need of you
And you walked away
So she asks me, after all that heart-full speech
Do you understand me, my friend?
I said, yes, I do understand you
Yet I still despise it
Because I am exactly the same.

This book, *Something Like Poetry – A Story of a Damaged Writer*, is a part of a series of three books that will be released soon after.

The second book will be titled *Poetry and Stitches – A Story of a Recovering Writer.*

The third book will be titled *Poetically Intact – A Story of a Healed Writer.*